Service Animals For Kids

Amazing Animal Books For Young Readers

By
Rachel Smith

Mendon Cottage Books
JD-Biz Corp Publishing

All Rights Reserved.

No part of this publication may be reproduced in any form or by any means, including scanning, photocopying, or otherwise without prior written permission from JD-Biz Corp

Copyright © 2015. All Images Licensed by Fotolia and 123RF.

Read More Amazing Animal Books

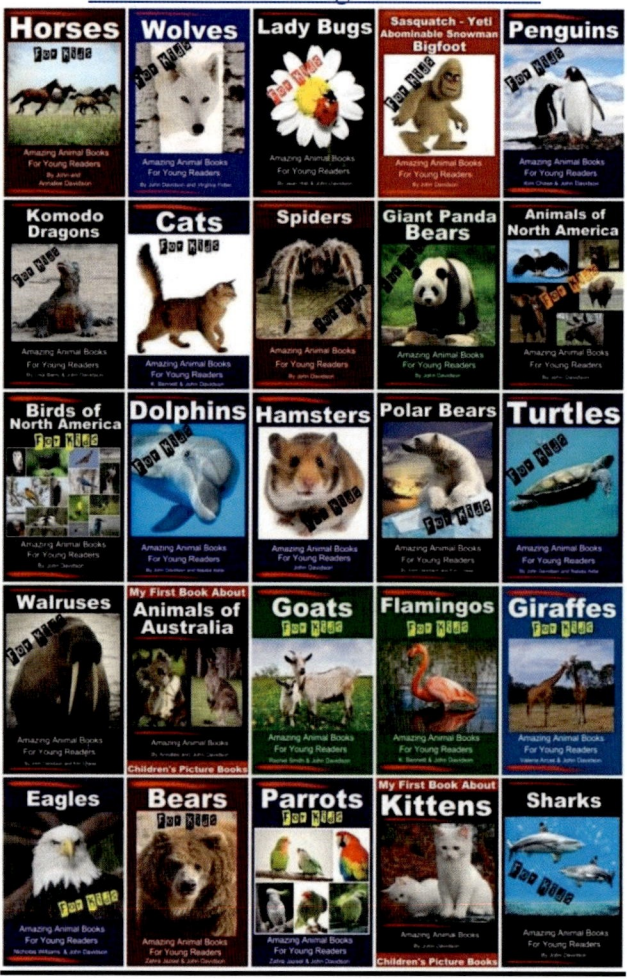

Purchase at Amazon.com

Table of Contents

Introduction 4

What is a service animal? 5

The history of service animals 8

Guide dogs 13

Hearing dogs 16

Psychiatric service dogs 19

Seizure dogs 21

Emotional support animals 23

Helper monkeys 25

Miniature horses as service animals 27

Conclusion 29

Author Bio 30

Publisher 31

Introduction

Service animals are a rare, but important, part of the disabled community. They allow people with disabilities of many different kinds to function normally, or at least independently.

There are many kinds of service animals throughout the world, though mostly the dog is used. They range from emotional support animals to seizure dogs to guide miniature horses. Even monkeys have been involved in the service animal world.

While there are many countries throughout the world that support the service animals and the people who need them, it is really a more recent thing and a lot of legislation involving them is hotly debated.

However, on the whole, service animals perform a great service to the community and their individual owners.

What is a service animal?

A service animal is any animal used to help a disabled person function normally.

A German service dog.

Service animals can include many kinds. Sometimes, they are called assist animals, assistance animals, or other names, especially in countries other than the United States of America.

For starters, there's the most well known kind: a seeing-eye dog. For a long time, the seeing-eye dog has been in use, helping blind people find their way around in unfamiliar areas. Most blind people don't have them, and use things like canes and counted steps, but the ones who do have them find them very valuable.

Another type is the hearing dog, or hearing animal. This is like the seeing-eye dog, but for deaf people. Their job is to pick up on dangerous sounds and help a deaf person navigate a hearing world.

Then, if we're going by three categories, there are all the other service animals. These help with all kinds of disabled folks, from mental illness to paralyzation and Parkinson's.

Now, most helping animals are dogs. Dogs are the most easily trained, and since they're not prey animals (animals that are eaten by other animals), dogs are less likely to be frightened by things and panic. Prey animals, on the other hand, have a built-in reaction to danger that is hard to get around. They tend to run, or otherwise panic a bit.

Dogs may be the most common animal, but is it not the only one. An emotional support animal can be many different kinds of pet animals. And there are such things as service miniature horses.

Miniature horses are mainly used as seeing-eye animals, to pull wheelchairs and the like, and sometimes as a support for a person with Parkinson's. Parkinson's is a disease that often affects older people; it slowly steals their ability to move and other things; they get quite wobbly, and get shaking hands. A miniature horse can be leaned on in times of instability.

Another kind of service animal is the helper monkey. This one is far more controversial than most types of service animals. Private groups train them to do things like open things for people, or turn knobs. They can even help wash hands and things like that.

The issue is that monkeys haven't been domesticated in the same way as other animals often used as service animals; the fear is that they will revert to their wild instincts and hurt someone or something. Another worry is that they will not be happy not being in the wild.

Animals also serve in things such as animal therapy. These are animals that are petted and such by people with mental illness or other mental disabilities; they are not considered service animals, but something separate.

The history of service animals

Service animals have been around longer than one would think. While the common use of service animals didn't happen until the early 20th century, one example in 1919 being when dogs were first used in animal therapy for psychiatric patients, the service dog at the very least has been around a very long time.

A blind man with his guide dog.

The most well known of the service animals is the guide dog. This is an animal that helps its blind owner get around. The image of a guide dog helping his owner has been around since Roman times, as discovered in a fresco (which is a kind of piece of art common in Ancient Rome). Such scenes have also been found in very old Chinese and European art.

Guide dogs as we know them began in the 1750s. This was when systems were beginning to be devised for training guide dogs; there was a blind Austrian man several decades later who trained his dogs so well that people believed he was faking being blind!

It was another Austrian that made one of the first manuals for training guide dogs around 1819. His manual instructs the user on what kind of harness to use, and also that the blind person should use a cane, Still, guide dogs were very much a European thing and not as common as could be hoped.

World War I was the birthplace of a big service dog movement. In Germany, many, many men who had been soldiers had been struck blind by mustard gas. Mustard gas, which is against international law to use in wars now, was developed as a gas attack, the first of its kind. It attacks the body, often blinding the victim and leaving them with mustard-colored blisters all over their body.

World War I was a horror on the world. Mustard gas was just one of the ways that what was then modern warfare was used on live people. Another example is the machine gun, first used in World War I, and the use of trenches.

But World War I did bring one good thing: a system that could be used for guide dogs.

This system was birthed by a German man who had trained collies to find wounded soldiers on the battlefield. The story goes that he left his German shepherd with a blind soldier, and when he returned, he noticed that his dog was protective of the soldier. So, he began a program in 1916 (which was before the war was over) to train German shepherds to guide blind people.

It didn't take off immediately. Because of the end of the war, bad things happened in Germany. They were blamed for the entire war, and forced to pay huge sums of money.

This caused extreme inflation. Inflation is when what was a dollar before is now ten dollars, even though it's the exact same thing. Inflation happens throughout the world at a slow rate, but in Germany, it happened very fast: people would wheel along wheelbarrows full of money just to pay for a small amount of food. People definitely did not have the money to pay for training a guide dog, so that program had to end.

Another association kept the training going, but by 1930, was not doing so well.

However, a Swiss woman discovered the program, and initially she was involved in training police dogs. Then, after she understood the program in depth in the 1920's, she became a passionate advocate for training guide dogs.

An American young man who was blind heard of what she said, and sent her a message that said he would come, get trained with the dog and bring it back to America, hopefully starting things there. He met her in Switzerland, and returned in 1929 to America with his trained dog, Buddy.

Shortly thereafter, the American school of seeing-eye dogs was started, and then a guide dog association kicked of five years later in England. The time of the guide dog had finally come.

Other types of dogs followed. Dogs were used to help veterans of World War II, who left the war with Post Traumatic Stress Disorder. PTSD is a psychiatric condition that means that people who had something frightening happen to them sometimes have difficulty. It means they relive the scary thing, or have nightmares, or startle really badly.

After that, hearing dogs, psychiatric service dogs, mobility assistance dogs, seizure dogs, autism dogs, and various other kinds followed. Other animals also followed, such as emotional support animals, helper monkeys, and service miniature horses.

The law in much of the international community is that public places must allow such animals to come into their business or other places. It is against the law in many countries to say a person can't come into, say, a restaurant with their guide dog. Schools also have to allow these animals in many countries.

In the United States of America, several laws have been passed to allow service animals in public places, housing, and other situations. In some laws, the service animal must be trained, even if it's just by the owner. In others, any animal that has been spoken for by a doctor as an emotional support animal is allowed these protections.

Some countries don't have these kinds of laws. In some places, it is entirely up to business owners or landlords if these animals will be allowed. In some of these countries, it's more likely that an animal will be permitted in the more tourism-heavy areas.

Guide dogs

Guide dogs are the first kind of service dog. They have been around for hundreds of years. They have been included in European literature since the Middle Ages, and shown in Ancient Rome and Medieval China as well.

A guide dog leading its human.

Guide dogs work with blind people, or people who can't see too well. Not all people who have guide dogs, or even all people considered blind, can see nothing at all. A lot of them are considered sight-impaired, such as someone who has lost patches of sight due to a disease than can affect older people, and other diseases and accidents. Some people are just born with very poor sight.

Unlike humans, dogs do not have complete color-sight. These dogs can't be taught to understand traffic signals and signs. But they can be taught to help their humans navigate to a place they already plan to go.

With getting somewhere, guide dogs are meant to do the small parts of navigating through, for example, a crowd, or busy streets. They make sure the human doesn't walk off the curb into traffic, or that they don't walk into people.

A blind person must have an idea of where they're going, even with a guide dog. Their cane is often also employed to check things in front of them.

The idea of how a guide dog leads their human is this: the human lays the plans, sort of like a person might use an online map to find directions to a place. The dog does the actual piloting; they follow the route. They do not get a say in the route.

Some of the most popular breeds for a guide dog are Labradors and golden retrievers. Another is the labradoodle, a cross between a Labrador and a poodle; this kind is good for people who are allergic.

The original kinds that were trained in Germany were collies adapted from work on the battlefield rescuing injured soldiers, and then German shepherds.

Shepherd dogs are still commonly used for guide dogs.

Hearing dogs

Hearing dogs are service dogs trained to help people who are deaf (can't hear) or are hard of hearing. There are a lot of dangers for a deaf person in a hearing world, and these dangers include things such as not hearing fire alarms, sirens, or other signs of danger.

A golden retriever. This kind of dog is especially known for making a good service dog.

However, hearing dogs are trained to help not just with emergencies, but with other sounds that deaf people need to know about. For instance, they can be trained to alert deaf people to someone calling their name, or something like a ringing telephone or an alarm clock going off.

A hearing dog is often tested for some things before they begin sound training. The key thing is to make sure that they are a good temperament, which is like a personality. You don't want a dog that's very jumpy, for example. You want one that will stay calm and do its job.

Another issue that could come up is a dog that refuses to work. Some dogs just aren't a good fit to be aware all the time of sounds that their human needs to hear. Something else may be whether or not they hear well too. You want a dog that can pick up sounds well.

So, when all these things are deemed okay, a dog will be trained for anywhere from three months to a year. Unlike a guide dog, they will simply be trained to hear sounds a deaf person can't; some also will look out for their human when out and about, so that something doesn't happen to them that they don't expect. Generally, the dog will be trained to alert the human to sounds, such as by nudging them.

It isn't the law in the United States of America that hearing dogs have to be trained by a professional to be legally a service dog and have the protections that all service animals have. Some deaf people train their own hearing dogs.

Like with guide dogs, Labradors, golden retrievers, collies, and other dogs are common as hearing dogs. It's much more unlikely to see a dog like a chihuahua, which is a very small dog that often has a bad temperament, as hearing dogs.

Psychiatric service dogs

Psychiatric service dogs, or psych dogs, are service dogs that help with psychiatric conditions.

A pit bull service dog. This breed is not as commonly chosen due to the bias against the pit bull, but they can make very good service dogs.

The question is, what is a 'psychiatric condition?'

For starters, there's PTSD, which has already been mentioned. Then there's schizophrenia, which is where a person believes, sees, or hears things that aren't real (this is an incredibly rare disorder).

There's also more common disorders such as depression and anxiety; depression means a person feels negatively most of the time, depending on the kind of depression, and anxiety means they feel very nervous all the time or about a specific thing.

A psych dog will do things like help a schizophrenic person realize what's not real when they're having a problem, or provide support to someone who is upset because of anxiety. They may move their human out of a stressful situation, or help them remember to take medication.

Psych dogs are not as well known as guide dogs and hearing dogs. They can be any size or breed, so they may be quite small indeed. Also, most of the time, people with psychiatric illnesses look like they're not disabled, even though they are. Some people are very shy about their mental illness, because other people can sometimes be mean to them about it.

So, people with psych dogs sometimes have trouble getting people to believe they need a service dog.

It's important to know that not all disabilities are obvious, and people with psychiatric illnesses, or mental illnesses, need their dog as much as other disabled people.

Seizure dogs

Seizure dogs, also known as seizure response dogs, are service dogs that make life liveable for people with severe seizure disorders. A seizure is when the electricity in the brain isn't right, and so the person's body shuts down for a few minutes. This can be scary for the person, and dangerous if they fall and hit their head.

This is a dog that is trained to help someone with diabetes; however, the training for seizure dogs has similarities.

A seizure response dog is trained to respond to seizures after they happen. They can do things like move their human to a safe place, get help, get medicine, help their human wake up to a safe and friendly face, and use an emergency response system.

These dogs make it possible for people who have fairly frequent seizures to go places that they might not be able to otherwise.

Another kind of seizure dog is the seizure alert dog. They can be trained to know when a seizure is about to happen in their human. However, there are people who don't believe this is actually possible, so they aren't as commonly used.

Emotional support animals

Emotional support animals are kind of like psych dogs. However, one of the big differences is that they are not usually trained.

An elderly man with his dog.

An emotional support animal can be any animal that helps a person with mental illness be relieved of some of their symptoms. This can mean calming a person with a psychotic episode or a panic attack, or it can mean keeping an autistic person content in an unfamiliar environment.

The way a pet is made an emotional support animal is through a doctor's recommendation. A doctor has to say that a person needs their animal for them to have the rights prescribed by law.

Emotional support animals are an American thing. They are protected under law to be able to move in to housing where pets aren't usually allowed, and they have a right to go to some places that other pets aren't allowed.

However, they don't have quite the same access as a trained service animal.

Helper monkeys

Helper monkeys are a kind of animal that is a bit more unusual. They aren't recommended by the Humane Society in America.

A capuchin monkey; this is a kind of monkey that is often used for the helper monkey programs.

A monkey can be trained in about seven years to do things for paralyzed people, or people with Parkinson's disease, for example. After being trained, they live about twenty-five to thirty-five years, far longer than a service dog.

These monkeys are usually trained to do things like open bottles and help their human wash their face. Because they have opposable thumbs, they can do a lot of things fully-functioning humans can do, though they are much smaller. They are usually trained to take care of themselves too, right up to washing themselves.

Helper monkeys are controversial (meaning, a lot of people have strong feelings about them on either side) because some think that their training is abusive. There is also the worry that they are more wild than dogs or other animals that have been kept by humans for thousands of years.

However, as of writing, there don't seem to be cases of helper monkeys hurting their humans.

Miniature horses as service animals

Miniature horses are a new sort of service animal. They live a good time, and they are small enough to do a lot of the things dogs do.

A regular size horse and a miniature horse. You can see the miniature horse is much smaller than a regular horse.

Because dogs are considered unclean by some religions, such as Islam, miniature horses have been proposed, and used, as a substitute. They can do a number of things.

For one, they can be mobility aides. Miniature horses, if properly harnessed, can pull wheelchairs for people who can't walk. This is one way the miniature horse can be a bit better than a dog.

Miniature horses are also used as guide animals. Like the guide dog, it helps its human, who is blind or sight-impaired, find their way around crowded or less safe areas. They use similar harnesses to guide dogs.

One of the downsides of a miniature horse as a service animal is that they need to be outdoors. So, the human who owns them must live in a more rural environment, such as a farm. Dogs can adapt to almost any environment, but the same is not true of miniature horses.

Miniature horses can live twice as long as dogs, and they are a good alternative for someone who's allergic or afraid of dogs, as well as for religious reasons.

Conclusion

Service animals make it possible for people with disabilities to live their daily lives without as much help. They can make them independent.

With the variety of animals known, and the ways we keep innovating, service animals will continue to be an integral part of many disabled people's lives for a long time to come.

Author Bio

Rachel Smith is a young author who enjoys animals. Once, she had a rabbit who was very nervous, and chewed through her leash and tried to escape. She's also had several pet mice, who were the funniest little animals to watch. She lives in Ohio with her family and writes in her spare time.

Publisher

JD-Biz Corp
P O Box 374
Mendon, Utah 84325
http://www.jd-biz.com/

Made in the USA
Coppell, TX
26 February 2024